William Babcock Weeden

Indian money as a factor in New England civilization

William Babcock Weeden

Indian money as a factor in New England civilization

ISBN/EAN: 9783744726887

Printed in Europe, USA, Canada, Australia, Japan

Cover: Foto ©Suzi / pixelio.de

More available books at **www.hansebooks.com**

JOHNS HOPKINS UNIVERSITY STUDIES
IN
HISTORICAL AND POLITICAL SCIENCE

HERBERT B. ADAMS, Editor

History is past Politics and Politics present History — *Freeman*

SECOND SERIES

VIII-IX

INDIAN MONEY

AS A FACTOR IN

New England Civilization

BY WILLIAM B. WEEDEN, A. M.

BALTIMORE

N. MURRAY, PUBLICATION AGENT, JOHNS HOPKINS UNIVERSITY

August and September, 1884

INDIAN MONEY

AS A FACTOR IN

NEW ENGLAND CIVILIZATION.[1]

COMMERCE abides by great waters, and the sea shore has been its natural home from very early times. New England owed much to the sea, and especially to the fish which her skilful hand drew from its deep waters; but there was a marine treasure, of the shore and already at hand, which has not received the attention due to it, in considering the development of our early history.

All new communities suffer for a currency. Capital must be scarce, but a circulating medium is yet rarer. The increasing wants of a new life constantly send off the valuable medium and tend to deprive enterprise and industry of the needed stimulus of money. This marine treasure was in the Indian money—" coyne, Monèash, from the English money," as Roger Williams[2] quaintly terms it. These beads made from sea shells strung, or embroidered, on belts and garments, were the coveted treasures of Indian life. Tradition gives to the Narragansetts the honor of inventing these valued articles, valuable both for use and exchange. This tribe was one of the most powerful, and it is asserted that their commercial use of wampum gave them their best opportunities of wealth. The Long Island Indians[3] manufactured the beads in large

---

[1] This paper was presented to the Historical and Political Science Association of the J. H. U. November 9, 1883, and is an important chapter in the Economic History of New England, to which Mr. Weeden is now devoting special attention.—ED.

[2] R. I. Hist. Coll. I., 1827, Key, p. 128.

[3] In this and other details I have freely used Dr. Woodward's interesting essay on Wampum, Albany, 1878.

quantities and then were forced to pay them away in tribute to the Mohawks and the fiercer tribes of the interior. Furs were readily exchanged for these trinkets, which carried a permanent value, through the constancy of the Indian desire for them. The holder of wampum always compelled trade to come to him.

Wampum a Legal Tender.

After the use of wampum was established in colonial life, contracts were made payable at will in wampum,[1] beaver, or silver. It is not the presence and free interchange of this shell currency, significant as it is, which chiefly interests us. This curious article, half natural, half artificial, getting its value from labor on the one hand and the desires fomented by the rude civilization of the barbarians on the other, played back and forth between the greedy Indian and the poor colonist for a long period. The use began in New England in 1627. It was a legal tender until 1661, and for more than three quarters of a century the wampum was current in small transactions. For more than a century, indeed, this currency entered into the intercourse of Indian and colonist, and therefore affected the whole development of that industry and commerce which we are studying. We must remember that, though Indian barbarities were cruel and destructive, they generally occurred on the frontiers. If we except the Pequot and Narragansett wars, the daily life of the settled portions of the colonies and provinces of New England was very little disturbed by Indian difficulties during long periods. In every day life, English and natives managed to live peacefully. The Indian was often brought into the colonial courts for minor offences, was fined, and generally paid his penalties when he had personal effects wherewith to pay. In 1673 the courts made him work out debts in daily labor. The Narragansett war was then gathering.

---

[1] 4 Mass. Hist. Coll., VII.

National and tribal civilizations have never dwelt long together. The political power of the nation necessarily dominates the lesser civilized force of the tribe, and finally subverts the race which lingers in the ruder form, however humane individuals of either polity may be.

WAMPUM AND INDIAN LABOR.

We have seen that money or currency is necessary to a new people. Another element is needed yet more. Labor[1] is a chief factor in civilized society[2] and the labor of the Indian[3] was made available through wampum. As Winthrop[4] shows, 10,000 beaver skins[5] annually came to the Dutch from the Great Lake. The chase was the primitive form of Indian industry and furs were the most conspicuous feature of foreign trade, as gold is to-day, but wampum played a much larger part in the vital trade of the time. Wampum, or the things it represented, carried deer meat and Indian corn to the New England men. Corn and pork went for fish; fish went for West India rum, molasses, and the silver which Europe coveted. West India products, or the direct exchange of fish

---

[1] E. Downing to Gov. Winthrop, 1637/8, 4 Mass. H. C. VI., p. 65: "I do not see how wee can thrive untill wee gett into a stock of slaves sufficient to doe all our business for our children's children will hardly see this great continent filled with people, soe that our servants will still desire freedom to plan for themselves, and not stay but for verie great wages."

[2] This was not so easily comprehended at first. Plymouth in 1646 repealed an order against employing Indians. Col. Rec., 1646, p. 64.

[3] "The Narragansetts, the most numerous people in those parts, the most rich also and the most industrious," . . . "they employed most of their time in catching of beavers, otters and musquashes, which they traded for English commodities, of which they make a double profit, by selling them to more remote Indians, who are ignorant." Wood's New Eng. Prospect, p. 2, ch. 3, 1634.

[4] I., 113.

[5] Cal. St. Papers, Colonial, 1660, p. 144. "It is reported that they have exported thence (Manhatan) to Holland this year, 1632, 15,000 beaver skins, besides other commodities." These were partly from New England.

with the Catholic countries of Europe, brought back the goods needed to replenish and extend colonial industries and trade.

The first contact with the hardy New England colonist benefitted the native Indian.[1] The fur trade has attracted most notice. But the steel hoe, substituted for a wooden or clam shell tool in the squaw's hand, must have produced more corn to the acre, and have afforded a surplus for trade. It went to the nearest market and, by the process indicated, increased quickly the productive wealth of the colonists.

The coastwise manufacture of wampum afforded a ready means of exchange which the colonists used at their trading posts with the distant Indians. The Indian dialect is meagre enough, but Roger Williams gives a good share of words and phrases which describe the manufacture, enumeration, and exchange of wampum. *Natouwómpitees*[2] quite trippingly "makes money or coyne;" another guttural signifies "to bore through," which term, before the English came, represented the passage of a stone drill. Afterward the unpronounceable *Puckwhegonnaútick*, "the awle blade sticks," shows the contact of the civilized tool[3] with the barbarian manufacture. If peltry was scarce, shells were always plenty and, for a long time, there was an almost unlimited demand for the genuine wampum. Alcohol, the fire water of the native, undid this benefit, but the process was gradual. The first influence of the incoming civilization was to quicken the Indian life proper, and to stimulate its barbarian labor to greater exertion, in order to obtain the largest share of the coveted civilized goods. In this view we have treated the Indian on

---

[1] Canonicus, in 1636, offered John Oldham, the daring Indian trader afterward murdered, Prudence or Chibacuwese Island in Narragansett Bay, if he would establish himself in trade there. Arnold, I., 8.

[2] Key, p. 131.

[3] "Six awl blades I pay to a native to carry to Ninigret and pray you to pay six more to him that brings them to you." R. Williams to J. W., Jr., at Pequot, 1648/9, Narra. Club, VI., 164.

his own ground, as a producer by his own methods. In other connections he enters as a porter, courier, and guide, as an occasional laborer, as an ally and friendly warrior, thus becoming a partial adjunct of the growing colonial life.

DEFINITION AND USES OF WAMPUM.

Wampum, or *wompam*, according to Trumbull was the name of the white beads made from stems or inner whorls of the *Pyrula Carica* or *Canaliculata* periwinkle shells so common on all the south coast of New England. When strung they were called *wampon* or *wampom*—*peage* or *peake* or *peg*, equivalent to "strings of white beads" for *peage* means "strung beads." Color was the basis of the nomenclature, as well as of the difference in value. *Wompi* was white; *Sacki* was black; *Suckaûhock* was the black beads made from the dark part[1] of the *poquaûhock*, the common quahog, *Venus' mercenaria* or round clam shell. The value of the black was generally twice that of the white. The original use of the words is not altogether clear; some contend that there was no generic word among the Indians signifying beads. The white was dyed sometimes to counterfeit black. The word[2] generally used among the Dutch who led in introducing the bead currency of the Indians, *Sewan* or *Zeewand* was more general in its application than wampum. But whatever the difficult Indian linguistic process may have been, the New

---

[1] "Toward anterior end is a deep purple or brownish—black scar indicating the point of muscular attachment—fishermen call it the eye." Am. Nat., XVII., 470.

[2] *Hiqua* consisted of strings of a mollusk (*Dentalium*) called by conchologists "tusk-shells," used in Br. Columbia, two inches and smaller. "The larger the size the greater the value; forty to the fathom was the standard, fifty to the fathom being worth scarcely half so much." Am. Nat., XVII., 476. "Wampum [*i. e., Hiqua*] however was *not* equally distributed [on the Pacific coast] any more than are riches in civilized communities—a point for communists to consider." Am. Nat., XVII., 479.

England men soon settled on wampum and peage as the working names for this currency.

The shell cylinders, black or white, were about one-eighth of an inch in diameter and one-quarter long. There were shorter beads used for ornaments, but there is hardly any trace of them in the currency. To bore these with a stone drill[1] was the work of a deft artisan, who must then polish them on stones in a weary round of labor, for all accounts agree that the finished product had a certain elegance of its own. It would interest us to know whether this work was done by the braves or the squaws. The beads were often used to pay the warriors for their services. Obedience was uncertain when an Indian sachem gave a command and he reinforced his authority by gifts. Canonicus says of wampum, "his wars keep him bare,"[2] and he says directly that he has paid his soldiers[3] in this currency as the colonists rewarded theirs. Roger Williams never mentions the women in connection with this work, as he does in describing those Indian operations which were carried on by the women exclusively. The product[4] was so highly prized and became so dignified by use in adorning the highest Indian personages

---

[1] "In the shell heaps along the New England Coast are hidden these old flint awls of prehistoric design, which may have been spun in some cases by a small bow such as jewelers employ at present." Lawson describes the drilling "which the Indians manage with a nail stuck in a cane or reed. Thus they roll it continually on their thighs with their right hand, holding the bit of shell with their left." Am. Nat., XVII., 471.

[2] R. Williams to Gov. Vane, 1637. Narra. Cl., VI., 26.

[3] Ibid., p. 58. "Canonicus replied that, though he and Miantonomo had paid many hundred fathoms to their soldiers us Mr. Governor did, yet he had not received one yard of beads nor a Pequot."

[4] Am. Nat., XVII., 468. "An Indian's utmost manufacture amounted only to a few pence a day; and all writers enlarged upon the great labor and patience needed to make it especially at the South. Hence, the purchasing power of a wampum bead was far in advance of that of a cowrie, the dentalium of the Pacific coast, or any other unwrought shell used as money." Ingersoll. Many archeologists believe fresh water shells found in mounds and graves were used for currency in the Mississippi valley.

that we may with reason imagine the braves themselves lending their doughty hands to bring out these works of art from Neptune's raw material. Natouwómpitea,[1] another inflection of the word we have cited, denotes "a coyner or minter." While it is probable that Williams carried the figure of coinage and the analogy of the mint too far in rendering the Narragansett sounds into English words, it is certain that the office or duty he describes had weight and importance among the natives. Every one made the beads at will; there was no seigniorage, nothing like our meaning of minting and coinage. But the terms Williams adopts to convey his notion of this business of making money show that it was not a mere menial labor, like the squaws' planting of corn or dressing of game.

WAMPUM BELTS.

The Indians strung the beads on fibres of hemp or tendons taken from the flesh of their forest meat. These strings were hung about the necks and wrists of the warriors and adorned their wives[2] and children[3] as well. They placed the beads under their heads when they slept.[4] The strings of *peage* were embroidered on strips of deer-skin making the *Máchequoce*, a girdle or belt "of five inches thicknesse,"[5] or more, and to the value of ten pounds sterling or more, which was worn about the waist or thrown over the shoulders like a scarf. More than ten thousand beads were wrought into a single belt four inches wide. These belts were in common use like the gold and jewelry of our day.[6] They also played the same

---

[1] R. W., Key, p. 130.

[2] "They (the cheefe ladies) weare a chaine of great pearls, or beades of copper, or smoothe bones, 5 or 6 fold about their necks bearinge one arm in the same." Hariot's Virginia, VIII.

[3] R. W., Key p. 131.

[4] Ibid., p. 52.

[5] Ibid.

[6] "A Sagamore with a humbird in his ear for a pendant, a black eagle in his occipit for a plume, a good store of *wampum-peage* begirting his loins,

symbolic part which survives in the crown jewels and other regalia of civilized nations. The kingly office betokened personal prowess and power, whether the incumbent was of Algonquin or Aryan lineage. When a superior sachem—the king of a later and higher civilization—took his seat, he must bear with him the evidence of power and the symbols of the love of his toiling subjects. The greater cross made the greater crown and each member of the tribe felt himself exalted by the emblems of dignity which his chieftain proudly bore in the rude assemblies of the aboriginal time. There must be wampum of the best kind and in abundance, just as the Czar at Moscow must have a gorgeous surrounding at his coronation.

The scene was pathetic when the Wampanoag Anawon surrendered Philip's regalia to Capt. Church in the fastnesses of Bristol County. The chieftain was dead. History has made him "King" Philip, to commemorate the heroism of his life and death. He almost made himself a king by his marvellous energy and state-craft put forth among the New England tribes. Had the opposing power been a little weaker, he might have founded a temporary kingdom on the ashes of the colonies. But the military science of Standish, the political wisdom of Winthrop, the steadfast endurance of English Puritans, the organized power of monied commerce and industry,—all these elements combined to create a national life too strong to be overcome by the personal prowess of Philip. Anawon was not obliged to surrender the wampum belts to Church. They were safely concealed and there was no demand for these articles so dear to the Indian in ordinary life. But Philip was gone, his power was broken, the headship and chieftaincy of his race had faded away in the stronger light of the incoming European's power.

---

his bow in hand, his quiver at his back, with six naked spatter lashes at his heels for his guard, thinks he is one with King Charles." Wood's New England Prospect, p. 66, 1634.

The most trusted warrior, councillor and friend of Philip went out quietly, brought the three or four wampum scarfs—splendid in his eyes—and gave them to his conqueror. The trinkets were not only valuable in themselves; they also symbolized and embodied a complete submission to the more mighty men, whose prowess had prevailed over the Indian. The largest scarf, nine inches wide, pictured with birds and beasts and flowers, when laid over the shoulders of the sturdy Rhode Islander swept his ankles. Another belt designed for the head carried two flags attached to it. Governor Winslow, in his letter to the king accompanying the spoils of Philip, speaks of them as "being his Crowne, his Gorge and two Belts of their own making of their goulde and silver."[1]

Gold it was not, coin it was not, but the governor correctly described it as "their gold." This quality gave it the attributes of a currency in the growing intercourse with the colonists. It was this quality, this costliness, which impressed the barbaric imagination and made the wampum a high symbol in every ceremony, political or religious. Whenever the Indians made an important statement in their frequent negotiations, they presented a belt to prove it, to give force to their words. "The hatchet fixed in the head"—one of the most forcible of their many figures, expressing a sense of wrong, a legitimate grievance—this hatchet must be removed by something more powerful than words. A belt was presented to discharge the grievance, and not by mere purchase. The value of the beads could hardly have been of consequence to a haughty confederacy like the Iroquois or Five Nations. It marked the gravity of the apology. It gave to the words the weight of hard physical facts and made the expressson an emblem of great force and significance.

The philologists call this literary office, this symbolic function of wampum, an elementary mnemonic record.[2] The same was fulfilled by the quippus, knotted strings or *quipu* of

---

[1] June 26, 1677. Arnold, I., 378. Citing original in B. S. P. O.
[2] Taylor, The Alphabet, I., 18.

the ancient Peruvians which were buried in their graves.[1] It is an ideogram in the bud; the expression of an idea by association to a mind which has not yet conceived those abstractions, we express through writing. "This belt preserves my[2] words" was a common remark of the Iroquois Chief[3] in council. It conveyed the words, giving warrant and sanction to the first communication, then preserved the facts by this symbolic association. The Iroquois were a mighty nation, almost an incipient state. Their only records[4] were in these mnemonic beads. To preserve them was a solemn office, and in important councils, the wampum keepers walked through the serried ranks of councillors reading from the belts the facts suggested to their memory. These facts had been "talked into" the beads, literally.[5] A mystic power animated the beads, thus quickened by the acts and deeds of this simple but intense savage life. The summons to war was in red or black, while peace messages were woven in purer white. When a communication excited anger, men kicked the belt about, in contempt, and a black belt accompanied words of condolence, becoming a sad token of mourning and sympathy.[6]

---

[1] Dawson, Fossil Men.

[2] Morgan, Ancient Society, p. 139.

[3] "Of wampum as a substitute for letters, we have as yet no trace in Europe." Dawson, Fossil Men, p. 144.

[4] "According to the Indian conception, these belts could tell, by means of an interpreter, the exact rule, provision or transaction talked into them at the time, and of which they were the exclusive record. A strand of wampum consisting of purple and white shell beads, or a belt woven with figures formed by beads of different colors, operated on the principle of associating a particular fact with a particular string or figure; thus giving a serial arrangement to the facts as well as fidelity to the memory. These strands and belts were the only visible records of the Iroquois; but they required those trained interpreters who could draw from their strings and figures locked up in their remembrance." A Sachem was Keeper, and he had two aids. Morgan, Ancient Society, p. 142.

[5] "Their most mysterious fabric was wampum." Parkman, Jesuits in North America, p. xxxi.

[6] Parkman's Pontiac I., pp. 145, 148, II., 272.

WAMPUM IN EXCHANGE FOR BEAVER.

We must consider these potent principles which lie at the base of all currencies, in estimating the character and influence of the intercourse between Indians and colonists which was regulated and sustained by wampum. Value in use, and value in exchange, both enter into the foundation of a currency.[1] The Long Island, Pequot and Narragansett tribes, had an article which was desirable in itself and which enforced a barter with those inland tribes rendering an equivalent to obtain it. .Barter began, but this did not constitute a currency. The article useful and desirable in itself, must have an essence of exchange, a force within itself which could compel not only that particular exchange but any exchange at the will of the owner.[2] This exchangeable quality was contributed by furs and especially by beaver. The colonist desired corn and venison, but all the world desired beaver. Wampum was the magnet which drew the beaver out of the interior forests. The beaver went to Europe; but the wampum remained, an equivalent value, as long as the Indian was a sufficient force in the rising colonial civilization, to maintain the circulation. The European possessed arms and gun-powder which far surpassed the ruder aboriginal

---

[1] The reverse principle prevailed recently on the Pacific coast, where it was hoarded, as a superior deferred value. On the Pacific coast "a young fellow sometimes procures it as an investment, laying away a few strings of it, for he knows that he cannot squander it at the stores; whereas if he really needs a few dollars of current cash he can always negotiate his shells with some old Indian who happens to have gold or greenbacks." Am. Nat., XVII., p. 479. Merchandise of any kind, even specie, may not inspire the local demand necessary in a good currency. We can see this in quite recent times. The Cowry *Cypraea Moneta*, a native of the Pacific and the Eastern seas, is used for money in Hindostan and many parts of Africa. In 1849 nearly 300 tons were imported into Liverpool and India ports, then exported for barter with the coast of Africa. Stearns, Am. Nat., III, 5.

[2] Some writers call the original use of wampum among the natives a currency. I think this is not a proper use of the word.

weapons, and he possessed stores of strange goods and wares, never imagined in aboriginal life. But he likewise possessed a talisman more potent than either or all of these things. Organized commerce could compel industry, could exact all the spasmodic labor possible to the barbarian. Fish, lumber, beaver, all equally desirable in Europe, could be obtained by the co-operation of the red men with the white. Wampum was the latent force which compelled the other products into action and kept up the equilibrium. Wampum had a certain dignity, which its usefulness, its exchangeable value, and ceremonial observance had engrafted upon it. It was a jewel, first used for personal adornment; then it became an emblem significant and powerful in all the phases of native life. They counted and cast it by a well developed and convenient system of numerals. By using grains of corn[1] to tally the calculation, they ran up into high numbers quickly and correctly. *Nquittômpscat*[2] was one penny, at six pence they condensed the inflected *Quttasháumscat* into *Quttauatu*.[3] At twelve pence, one shilling, with the same process they dropped the agglutinating numeral, denominating it *neen*,[4] that is two sixpences. At five shillings the long word changes again into *Piúckquat* which equals ten sixpences. *Piñck* meaning ten. "This *Piúckquat* being sixtie pence, they call *Nquittômpeg*, or *Nquitnishcaŭsu*, that is one fathom,

---

[1] R. W., Key, p. 42.

[2] Since writing out my view of Williams' measures, Hon. J. Hammond Trumbull has favored me with the following and other suggestions: "The unit of measure, as he gives it, is *ompscat* or *aumscat*, which Eliot and Williams both use as the Indian equivalent for a 'penny.' This word seems to have originally denoted a span, or a hand's breadth; though I am not quite certain of this. Eliot in Matt., 20: 2, wrote *nequt-omskot* (-*nquit-tômpscat* of Williams) for a 'penny.' To this name or measure all the values given in Williams' table are referable."

[3] So he says, they call two sixpences "their *quttauatues-neèn*, which seems to stand for a 'couple' or 'double.'" Trumbull.

[4] A form of the simple numeral *Neèsse* two.

five shillings."[1] *Nquittemittànnug* was one thousand, and *Nquitpausuckéemittánug* was one hundred thousand.

Williams' system of enumeration was written down, after this long process of trade I have described had worked itself into custom, and had been defined in law. His Indian words, as well as his translations, are names of operations, which had been going on before his eyes, for a dozen years or more. They are the results of mutual intercourse. How much is strictly aboriginal, and how much came from his own consciousness, we can never know.

UNIT OF MEASURE AND UNIT OF VALUE.

The unit of measure,[2] first used among the natives, had no closer connection with an English foot than twelve linear inches have to do with the foot on which the European stands. The cubit was used among the Iroquois in early transactions, and we wonder that the New England men did not put it among the remarkable evidences of prophecy, by which they fondly identified the North American natives with the ten lost tribes and the old testament of the Hebrews. This unit of measurement was customary in aboriginal traffic and extended from the end of the little finger to the elbow joint. Probably the standard came from the easy process, which catches the string of beads in the first knuckle of the little finger, runs it down the forearm and marks at the elbow with the other hand; then it hangs the elbow mark on the

---

[1] "Many, probably all Indian tribes had names of measure corresponding more or less nearly to the English *inch, span, foot, cubit* and *fathom*, but none of these names are used in Williams' list of wampum values, except ómpscat." Trumbull.

[2] Says Lindstrom in New Jersey, in 1640: "Their way of trying them is to rub the whole thread full on their noses; if they find them full and even, like glass beads, then they are considered good, otherwise they break and throw them away. Their manner of measuring their strings is by the length of their thumbs; from the end of the nail to the first joint makes six beads." Am. Naturalist, XVII., 468.

knuckle, repeating the operation rapidly and at will. It was literally a handy[1] method of measurement. In theory a short man was equal to a long one, like the custom of our modern tailors in selling a suit. But the North Americans were shrewd as well as cautious, and the slow Dutch complained that when a trade came to final adjustment, the tallest aboriginal man appeared to measure and receive the wampum. Apparently this unit of measure merged into the unit of count or value, as easily as the English pound of the currency changes from weight to value. We hear nothing of this cubit as a measurement in any recorded transactions with the Indians, after the period[2] when wampun attained the dignity of a legal currency.

THE FATHOM OF WAMPUM.

The fathom was a name for a count, an enumeration of beads. "This *Piúckquat* being sixtie pence, they call *Nquit-tómpeg*, that is one fathom, five shillings."[3] Sixty pence, the fathom of beads, was more or less, according to the number of beads allowed by the statute to be equivalent to a penny. If the number was six, then the fathom was 360, but if it was four, as under the Massachusetts standard of 1640, then the fathom numbered 240 beads. We are not to forget that this was a fluctuating standard of value. The tributes of the Indian tribes to the colonists were usually payable in

---

[1] Am. Nat., XVII., p. 477. Quite recently "among the Hupas in Oregon, nearly every man had ten lines tatooed across the inside of his left arm, about half way between the wrist and the elbow; in measuring shell-money he drew one end over his left thumb nail, and if the other end reached to the uppermost of the tattoo lines, the five shells (in 1873) were worth $25 in gold or even more."

[2] "The Capt's (Atherton's) demand was 300 fathoms for the debt, and 200 for this expedition. They paid 140, and said it was the whole, and that the difference was made by the measure," that is by the count. R. W. to J. W., Jr., Oct. 17, 1650, Nar. Cl., VI., 203.

[3] R. W., Key, p. 129.

fathoms. Contracts for the sale of lands were made by the Indians for considerations of all kinds, wampum, coats, guns, bullets, and wares of all sorts. The island of Conanicut in Narragansett Bay was sold to Coddington and his associates in 1657 for "one hundred pounds in wampum peage."

The unit of the fathom[1] of wampum brought it into correlation with the other currencies used in the colonies. The beads were at first worth more than five shillings a fathom, the price at which they passed current when Williams wrote in 1643.[2] A few years before, the fathom was worth nine or ten shillings. But beaver fell in England,[3] and that reduced the price of wampum in the colonies. The wampum was virtually redeemable in beaver, as these changes of value show. As long as the natives were active and furs were plenty, there appears to have been no difficulty in passing any quantity of wampum in common with other currencies. The Bay annulled its statutes, making the beads a legal tender in 1661.[4] Rhode Island and Connecticut followed this example soon after. In 1667,[5] the conspiracy of Philip with the Narragansetts and other powerful tribes, was reported and became a grave cause of uneasiness in all the colonies. We can see the vacillating policy of the Plymouth colonists in their statute against selling powder and shot to the natives. It was repealed in 1665, re-enacted in 1667, and repealed again in 1669. It was not because the Indian's wampum was refused that he began to conspire and finally

---

[1] R. W., Key, p. 129.
[2] Ibid.
[3] The fall of beaver in England probably occurred between 1635 and 1640. In 1630, according to Felt, they failed in regulating the price for colonial trade at 6s. per pound. Freed from the artificial regulation, it rose to 10s. @ 20s. Gov. Bradford says, coat beaver was fully 20s. in 1634, and Belknap puts common at 12s. in N. H., the same year, 1635. Felt makes the price 10s. 1638, Connecticut Colony rates it at 9s. In 1640, the price was 6s. to 8s. in Casco, Me.
[4] Rec. Mass., IV., part 2, pp. 4, 5.
[5] Arnold, R. I., I., 331.

fought unto extermination. But, as he ceased to be useful, he had to fight, and the relegation of his precious toil-won beads to the rank of common commodities marks the decline of the savage in New England life. The men of Rhode Island said in 1662, of the article in question that "it is a commodity."[1] It was always that and nothing more. It continued in common use for more than half a century after its lawful tenor was changed.

The colonists would not have been more reluctant to receive it in 1660 than in 1640, if the same facility of redemption had existed, if its final value had remained certain, for its continued use as an accessory currency shows that it was convenient and desirable. Labor had become better organized; corn was more abundant among the colonists; furs[2] were more remote and inaccessible. The poor Indian had become a worse savage and not a better civilized man; above all, the improving civilization of the colonies had outgrown him. It had left him struggling like a fish in the tide falling on the strand. There is not water enough to help him to swim, there is enough to keep him gasping for life. The statute only marks the date of the social change. It does not change the essential nature of wampum, beaver or silver.

INDIAN TRADE OF PLYMOUTH AND MASSACHUSETTS.

In 1627 De Rasières[3] with a Dutch trading vessel came into Plymouth from New Amsterdam. In her cargo was a

---

[1] "It cannot but be judged that it is but a commodity, and that it is unreasonable that it should be forced upon any man." R. I. Col. Rec., 1662, I., 474.

[2] As early as 1645, Johnson declares the beaver trade outgrown at Springfield, Mass., "fitly seated for a Beaver trade with the Indians, till the merchants encreased so many that it became little worth, by reason of their out buying one another, which hath caused them to live upon husbandry." Wonder Working Providence, p. 199.

[3] Palfrey, I., 238, cites De Rasières' letter written to the Hague. "They have built a Shallop [at Manomet on Buzzard's Bay] in order to go and

lot of wampum valued at £50, for the Dutch had learned its
uses as a currency in their traffic with the natives. They
sent this first instalment to the trading post on the river
Kennebec, where it was kept in hand for two years.[1] Meanwhile the interior Indians heard of it, and the assured supply
brought a demand. For some years after, the Plymouth men
could hardly furnish wampum enough,[2] and the control of
this currency gave them an advantage which virtually
excluded the fishermen and other traders from competing
for the trade of the river. They obtained constant supplies
from Connecticut,[3] and probably from Long Island and Narragansett. In 1634[4] Winslow was enabled to send twenty
hogsheads of beaver[5] to England, nearly all of which had
come through an exchange of wampum. In 1637[6] the trade
in maize with the Indians up the Connecticut river was so
important to the Colonies below, that they recorded an ordinance with penalties restricting it. No man was allowed to
go among them or to make any public or private contract of
any kind, lest "the market for corne may be greatly advanced
to the prejudice of these plantacons." In 1638[7] the same

---

look after the trade in Sewan in Sloup's Bay [an inlet of Narragansett
Bay] * * * which I have prevented for this year by selling them 50
fathoms of Sewan, because the seeking after sewan by them is prejudicial to us, inasmuch as they would, by so doing, discover the trade in
furs; which if they were to find out, it would be a great trouble to us to
maintain.

[1] Baylies' Hist. Plymouth, I., 151.
[2] Bradford, Hist. Plymouth, p. 234.
[3] Baylies, Plymouth, I., 48.
[4] The first recognition of the beads as money, I find was in 1634, when
the Patrons represented to the Assembly at Hague that Sewan being in a
measure the only money of the country be permitted. O'Callaghan, New
Neth., p. 161.
[5] From 1631 to 1636 they sent to England 12,530 Beaver and Otter.
Coat beaver sold at 20s. to 24s. per pound, the skin at 14s. to 16s. Bradford,
Hist. Plym., p. 346, Mass. II. C.
[6] Col. Rec. Conn., 1637, p. 11.
[7] Col. Rec. Conn., 1638, p. 18.

authority[1] fixed the price of corn brought in by any one—except Mr. Pynchon at Springfield, with whom there was a special contract—at 5s. 6d. per bushel in money, at 6s. per bushel in wampum at 3 a penny, or if in beaver according to the order at 9s. per pound. All the variations and comparative values of currencies in the colonial transactions are interesting, and I can only refer to them here. This particular instance shows that wampum had then made itself nearly equal in purchasing power to money of any kind. The Bay authorities[2] had fixed the rate in 1637[3] at six beads for a penny for any sum under 12d. In the early statutes only one rate is mentioned. Probably it was understood that the black was included at double the rate fixed for the white. In many of the later laws, the two colors are mentioned in that proportion. The usual difficulty caused by a standard of value fluctuating between different markets was experienced now. Connecticut received wampum for taxes in 1637[4] at four a penny. They tried to bring it to the Massachusetts standard, for the ordinance of 1640[5] says "the late order concerning Wampū at sixe a penny shall be dissolued, and the former of fower a penny and two pence to be paid in the shilling shall be established." In the same year Massachusetts[6] came to the Connecticut standard, the white to pass at four and the "bleuse" at two a penny, not above 12d. at a time, except at the will of the receiver. In 1641[7] they submitted to the inevitable and made the shell beads a legal tender at six a penny in sums of £10.

---

[1] And at Plymouth, 1636–7, certain persons "did contrary to the ancient laws of this colony, trade with the Indians for corne," one-half the penalty was remitted and half the forfeited corn returned to them. Pl. Col. Rec., I., 50.

[2] In 1636 "the trade of beaver and wampum was to be farmed and all others restrained from trading." Winthrop, I., 193.

[3] Mass. Rec., I., 238.

[4] Col. Rec. Conn., 1637, p. 12.

[5] Col. Rec. Conn., 1640, p. 64.

[6] Rec., I., p. 329.

[7] Rec., I., 302.

Evidently the proud merchants and capitalists of the Bay had adopted the Indian money, only when the absolute necessity of their community demanded the sanction of law. The precious maize which many writers have designated as an essential factor in the prosperity of the early colonists had yielded the first place, and shell money became the principal medium of intercourse with the natives. Stringent necessity forced men like Winthrop and Endicott to receive these barbaric trinkets on a par with solid coin of the old English realm. Englishmen learn late, but they learn thoroughly. The coin marks, the £ s. d. of their money, they adopted from the Lombard merchants who settled in London, and taught them the larger commerce. They brought these mystic symbols of civilization across the seas and stamped them on the shell treasures of Canonicus and Sassacus.

This currency reveals to us through its vagaries, two aspects of colonial life. (1), The intercourse with the natives which was so important a factor in developing the opportunities of wealth in the infant settlements of New England; (2), the growing wealth and traffic of these communities, which were forced to use the aboriginal currency, yet were constantly tending to throw it off and substitute the more current and universal silver which flowed in from the increasing West India trade about the middle of the century. The standard, even after it was recognized by law, was always fluctuating. Probably the colonists never fully believed in its value or permanency, and kept it for as brief periods and in as small amounts as possible. It circulated literally. Once I heard an inn-keeper remark that he never scrutinized the bank bills offered by his customers, too closely. But "we put the doubtful ones on the top of the layer in our till: and at the end of the season we never have any bad money on hand." The ethics of this practice may be matter for argument, but there is not the slightest doubt that it stimulates trade.

REGULATION OF THE CURRENCY.

The legislators tinkered at the money question constantly. In 1640,[1] the Bay adopts four a penny for the white, and two for the blue. In 1641,[2] this was changed to six a penny, and the beads were made lawful money for any sum under £10. This year the trade was farmed out and one of the conditions obliged the lessees to redeem from Harvard College all accumulations of wampum in its treasury under £25. In 1642,[3] the rate was six a penny in Connecticut. This year the farmers of the beaver trade in the Bay were ordered to give an account of the wampum.[4] The £10 allowance instituted in 1641, lasted only two years, for we find that in 1643,[5] "it shall passe, but to the value of —." Unfortunately this amount is left blank in the record. Doubtless it was found in Boston, the central market of exchange, that shabby debtors availed themselves of this legal privilege to force the Indian currency into transactions where the ordinary and customary usage of trade would not admit it fairly. £10 was quite a large sum in the every day transactions of that period. Apparently this change of legal status did not affect the current use of this money throughout the New England colonies, as well as other districts.

Wampum had become a universal currency, exchangeable for merchandise, for labor, for taxes. By 1645,[6] the inventories of deceased colonists commonly contained items of peage, and frequently there was no other money. The story was that in 1647,[7] an old English shilling was picked up in the highway at Flushing, Long Island. It was so great a

---

[1] Mass. Rec., I., 302.
[2] Ibid., I., 329.
[3] 1642, Col. Rec. Conn., p. 79.
[4] Rec. Mass., II., 27.
[5] Ibid., p. 48.
[6] Felt's Mass. Currency, p. 27.
[7] Thompson, Long Island, II., p. 11.

curiosity that the public attention was attracted, many never having seen a similar coin. Judgments[1] of the courts were made payable in shell money. Wild animals, wolves and bears especially, were a serious impediment to agriculture. The rewards offered for their destruction generally went to the Indians; often these were made payable to the natives directly, by the terms of the ordinance.[2] The Dutch in New York had hardly any other effective currency in the smaller sums, and it was common in New Jersey and Pennsylvania.

Decline of Wampum.

In 1644 the Indian trade was at its height in New England, if we may judge from the action of the United Colonies.[3] The Commissioners endeavored in vain to create a large corporation of share holders, with ample funds and numerous agents to work this traffic by systematic methods. The Bay[4] orders this proposition to be "established and confirmed for

---

[1] Col. Rec. Conn., 1649, p. 193.

[2] Thompson, Long Island, I., 470.

[3] Winthrop, 1644, II., 160. Palfrey thinks Winthrop refers to the scheme of Corporation for Indian trade in the United Colonies. Boston merchants saw great trade in beaver, coming from the North-West. They "petitioned the court to be a company for that design, and to have the trade which they should discover to themselves for 21 years. The Court was very unwilling to grant any monopoly but perceiving that without it, they would not proceed, granted their desire." In 1643 or 1642 there was "great store of beaver" from Boston for London. Winthrop, II., 150.

1644, Jt. Stock Co. for Indian trade. "This scheme appears to have originated in Massachusetts. (Mass. Rec., 60. Comp. Win., II., 160.) I do not know that anything came of it, though Connecticut agreed to engage in it, 'if other jurisdictions do the like.' Plymouth declined on account of insufficient means, as well as of doubts about its success."

Palfrey, II., 152. Plym. Rec., II., 82.

1644. "The propositions of the Commissioners concerning a general Indian trade (except corne, fishe and venison) is also approved and settled by the Court, vppon the terms therein propounded, if other jurisdictions doe the like." Col. Rec. Conn., I., 113.

[4] Mass. Rec., II., 86.

ten years." No changes were registered in the legislation until 1649, when the receipt of wampum in the Massachusetts was forbidden for taxes or "to country rate."[1] But in the same year the same authority ordained that, "it shall remayne passable from man to man."[2] When the State puzzles over a rickety currency, a common device is to pass it out, and refuse to pass it in. We cannot ascertain certainly whether the fluctuations in the value of the beads or the rating per penny noted in the statutes were occasioned by an over supply of the article, or by other causes. Probably many causes combined to change the faith of the merchants in this barbaric medium. During our civil war, the legal tender notes of the United States fluctuated violently in their gold value; the changes were often illogical and the causes were hard to trace. I think it is clear that, as the colonist increased, the native had less relative power in maintaining his own money. In the early statutes the Indian is not mentioned as differing from other persons in the exchange of wampum, whether for receipt or payment. There was no occasion to single him out, while the red man had corn, furs, and meat in plenty. All men were then economically free and equal before the law. In 1644 as we have seen, the trade with him received the best attention and called forth all the energies of the State. By 1649[3] his money dropt from the tax gatherer's list, and the aboriginal man is no longer financially equal to the European intruder as we shall farther see.

Roger Williams reflects the anxiety prevailing in the native mind when he asks the younger Winthrop whether "the *peag* will be sold at under rates."[4] To understand this fully, we

---

[1] Ibid., 167, May 16, 1649, also II., 279, May 2, 1649.
[2] Mass. Rec., III., p. 153.
[3] In 1655 the Colony allowed to the Treasurer £35.10 for peag burnt with the Treasurer's house, showing that it was still in circulation in Massachusetts. Felt, Mass. Currency, p. 37.
In 1659 Rehoboth makes a town contract for £8, payable in wampum. Bliss, p. 48.
[4] R. Williams' letter, March, 1648/9, Nar. Cl., VI., 171.

must consider the relations of the two governments, Indian and Colonial. The shrewd administrators of the United Colonies had devised a scheme by which the native, while being improved off the face of the land, should pay in money for the protection of that paternal government, which gently, piously, but firmly did the work. The Wampanoag, Narragansett, Pequot and other tribes agreed to pay, and often did pay substantial tributes in wampum to the various authorities in the United Colonies, which were able to exact them. This matter of tribute has created much discussion, and the equity of these transactions has been seriously questioned. If any one can discover a universal standard of justice between opposing civilizations, he will be able to render a final verdict in this question, as well as other Indian problems. In this same year, Williams continuing the sentence cited above that *Punhommin* coming from the Bay reports that "they must pay great black at thirteen to the penny, and small black at fifteen, and white at eight. I tell them last year it was measured, and so word was sent to me they should pay it by measure." Probably the rate of depreciation was exaggerated, for at other times Roger[1] freely and forcibly expressed his conviction that his native friends could not be depended upon. It will be noted that, in the violent fluctuations of value in the beads going on at Boston, which this report shows, both parties were forced to abandon the unit by count in pennies, and go back to the unit of measure in settling tribute. The terms of the tribute were almost always stated in fathoms of wampum, but Williams' correspondence would indicate that sometimes the payment was made by count,[2] or market value and sometimes by measure.

Rhode Island and Providence were more affected by the Indian community than all the other colonies, for many

---

[1] "All Indians are extremely treacherous." To Gen. Ct. Mass., 1654, Nar. Col., VI., 276.
[2] "In 1649 Ninigret alledged that about 600 fathom was payed by measure which he accompted by tale wherein ther was a considerable difference." Hazard, H. C., II., 131.

reasons. The circumstances of their foundation, their weakness and location amid the most powerful tribes, the friendly intercourse of Williams and their leaders with the sachems,— all these facts combined to enforce harmonious relations with the diminishing aboriginal power. Accordingly the Rhode Island statute,[1] made only two months later, shows that they made the Indian equal to the colonist, and kept his money at better rates than prevailed in Boston.

COUNTERFEIT WAMPUM.

When wampum commanded the market and was most available, much trouble was occasioned by the introduction of bad, counterfeit, and ill-made beads. The Indian, always a cautious and astute trader, knew the article best, and would refuse any but regular specimens. This compelled the colonists to struggle with the inferior portion, which had no value for them, except as a medium of exchange. Massachusetts ordered in 1648,[2] that it "shall be intire, without breaches, both the white and the black without deforming spotts." And they now instituted a process more like coinage than any thing which Williams found among the Indians, and described in the familiar terms of the mint. They enacted that the beads should be properly strung into eight

---

[1] Noe person within this Collonie, after the tenth of June next, shall take any black peage of the Indians, but at four a penny; and if any shall take black peage of the Indians under four a penny, he shall forfeit the said peage, one-halfe to the informer, and the other halfe to the State." R. I. Col. Rec., I., 217.

May 23, 1649. Roger Williams gives a version of this law differing from the plain construction of it. He says to J. Winthrop, Jr., "one law passed (at Warwick), that the natives should no longer abuse us, but that their black should go with us as with themselves at four a penny." Nar. Cl., VI., 180, May 26, 1649. His motive may have been to impress on Winthrop that the Providence Colony would not be too favorable to the natives, as the United Colonies were pressing them for tribute.

[2] Mass. Rec., III., 146.

known parcels: 1d. 3d. 12d. 5s. in white; 2d. 6d. 2s. 6d. and 10s. in blacke. This made a complete series of "change." This was in consequence of the suggestion of President Dunster, of "the College at Cambridge," who had in the same year called the attention of the Commissioners of the United Colonies to the matter of bad, false and unfinished peage, recommending the General Courts to remedy it. Connecticut in 1649,[1] ordains that it be "strunge, and in some measure strunge sutably, and not small and great, vncomely and disorderly mixt, as formerly it hath been." The loose and imperfect, driven from New England, went West and passed at a slight discount in New Netherlands, aggravating the difficulties already existing there. No currency can maintain its functions, unless it is sustained by some community or body of a community which believes in its value, and with sufficient ability to uphold the conviction. As already intimated,[2] the time must come when the power of the native, as an economic agent and producer in the mixed colonial society, must fail. This occurred in 1661 and 1662, when all the New England colonies ceased to receive wampum as a lawful currency.

SURVIVAL OF WAMPUM.

This action did not drive it out of circulation. It had a *quasi* legal foundation long after.[3] In 1666[4] Connecticut grants

---

[1] Col. Rec. Coun., 1649, p. 546.
[2] See previous portion of this monograph.
[3] Rhode Island recognizes it in Statutes,
   At six per pen. 1655, R. I. C. R., I., 308.
   " eight " 1658, for court fees, I., 400.
   " six " 1659, " " I., 412.
   " sixteen " 1670, " fines, II., 297.
In 1669 Long Island Indians paid Ninigret five pounds tribute in peage at six a penny. Ibid., II., 270.
[4] Col. Rec., Conn., 1666, p. 52.

"to Norridge 50 fathom of *Wompom* or the effects thereof." According to the reports of a renegade white, Philip[1] failed in some of his projected arrangements for ammunition in his great campaign, because New England money would not pass with the French as readily as wampum or beaver. New York continued the beads in circulation longer than the regular use prevailed in New England. In 1693 they were recognized in the definite rates of the Brooklyn ferry.[2] They continued to be circulated in the more remote districts of New England through the century, and even into the beginning of the eighteenth. Madame Knight found "Wampom[3] viz., Indian beads which serves for change," classed as money in Connecticut in 1704.[4] She notes definitely that it was current with silver, and was not in the class of "country pay," which included provisions and other produce.[5]

Results of the Use and Disuse of Wampum.

The use and disuse of wampum indicated in these pages shows that: (1.) There was an intimate intercourse of white and red men in colonial life during half a century, which largely increased the resources of the new community. (2.)

---

[1] Nart. Cl., VI, 382-167. R. Wms. to Gov. Leverett.
[2] "In 1693, the ferriage of each single person from New York to Brooklyn was eight stivers in wampum, or a silver two pence. Further than this we are unable to trace, though we have good reason to believe that it circulated to a limited extent, for sometime thereafter." Woodward, Wampum, p. 58.
[3] Journey Ed., 1865, p. 56.
[4] "Kalm saw it among the Hurons and also below Quebec in 1748. So slow, in fact, were the red men to relinquish this currency, that wampum continued to be fabricated until within fifty years in several towns of New York State (chiefly at Babylon, L. I.) to meet the demand for it by western fur-traders." Am. Nat., XVII, 476.
[5] Am. Nat., XVII, 475. In 1673, when the true wampum had become very scarce, owing to the hoarding of it by the Indians and its disposal to remote tribes, "the Dutch council, therefore, issued an edict advancing its legal value twenty-five per cent."

After the commercial, industrial, or purely economic element in this life had worked itself out, there was little wholesome or prosperous intercourse between the two races. (3.) The efforts of the colonists to turn the natives to another civil and religious system, to tear them out of aboriginal life and plunge them into the Hebrew-European living of the new comers,— to civilize them into copper-colored Puritans—failed, and from the nature of the case must have failed.

The first proposition proves itself in the facts, we have already seen. The second is sufficiently apparent in the decay of the great aboriginal trade which culminated about 1645 in the declining export of beaver and aboriginal products, in the growing export of the products of colonial agriculture and industry. These are the homely economical features of the life of the time. There are some larger lineaments of humanity, which the history of the epoch tortures into tragedy, and stains with blood, shed by infamous treachery. We may only allude to the peaceful life and death of Canonicus of Narragansett, of Chickataubut of the Massachusetts, and of Totanimo of Connecticut, contrasted with the melancholy end of Miantonomo and the tragic death of Philip, to illustrate the good and the ill of that momentous contact of races on New England soil. Philip met death after a manly struggle, which any Aryan or Indian might be proud to have made. But no descendant of Bayard or Sydney, and especially no Rhode Islander can read the story of Miantonomo,[1] without that tingling of the blood which sends pain through his fingers, and that melting in his eyes which sends a thrill to his heart. Winthrop found a

---

[1] "In all his answers he (Miantonomo) was very deliberate and showed good understanding in the principles of justice and equity, and ingenuity withal. He demanded that his accusers might be brought." Winthrop, II., 80. "None has been so painful in the whole progress of my labours, as this which relates to the treatment of Miantunnomoh by our fathers. Such a case of perfidy, or cruelty, or both, it is impossible to pass without animadversion." Mr. Savage's note. Winthrop, II., 133.

man in the noble savage, and his candid editor, after the softened life of two centuries, calmly admits and regrets that fierce treachery, which animated the New England men in this horrid affair. These astute men of the United Colonies, more cunning than Uncas, sacrificed the friendly Miantonomo for the good of the State, as they conceived it. Yet it was not that larger necessity which has sometimes forced leaders to do an immediate wrong for the ultimate good of the whole. They killed the native Prince in a theologico-political delusion, in a hunt after the heterodoxy of Gorton at Warwick. It was not even a direct punishment of heresy. It was, as Mr. Savage[1] suggests, the slaughter of an innocent man of another race and different religion, because he had dared to befriend the believers in an anti-Puritan dogma. The sad death of Miantonomo was comparatively early in the mixed aboriginal and colonial life we have been treating. But the principle which animated it, belongs to the essence of our main proposition. If Miantonomo had been false, if the Commissioners at Hartford had been more humane, if Philip[2]

---

[1] Winthrop, II., 134, ed. 1826.

[2] It adds little to the magnificent work of Dr. Palfrey to say that his conclusions, in his statement of native and colonial conflicts, are on the whole well-grounded. But his view of Philip is hardly consistent with itself. He describes him "with a strenuous purpose, a capacity for political combination, and an aptness for influencing the action of men, such as belong to minds of a high class, he slowly matured a conspiracy," &c. &c. (III., 222). This is all that one would claim for him now, and it is all that he could have been, if the present writer's view of the two civilizations be correct. In combating Hubbard and the later writers, he rates Philip too low politically. The inconsistent details in Palfrey's picture proceed from the tacit assumption that the native ought to have been a better convert to the colonial system of living, of civil government, and of worship. He admits "it were to be wished that the Colonists had borne their superiority with more meekness." (III., 218, note). But this in the small type of the notes. The humane side of the story is written small while the political necessity is in the larger expression of the text. And he says, "He (the Indian) was not ready, it is true, to be transformed from a hunter into a herdsman." (III., 140). I presume he means an agricultural herdsman. That is

had been less bold and sagacious, the final result would not have been different substantially. " Canonicus, the old high Sachim of the Narragansett Bay, (a wise and peaceable Prince) often repeated this word Wunnaunewayeán, Englishman." " If the Englishman speaks true, if hee means truly, then shall I goe to my grave in peace, and hope that the English and my posteritie shall live in love and peace together,"[1] says Roger Williams.

CONFLICT OF RACE.

It was not a matter of morals, as this gentle natured son of the forest fancied. Good intentions mitigate, but they cannot avert the inevitable conflict between races in different stages of civilization. While the conflict was in abeyance, the better individuals of both races tried to keep the peace and to maintain the best concord possible. On the one side was a rude system of justice administered through the courts by due process of law; on the other, private war and the blood feud were not only allowed by the totem system, but they rested

---

always true, for there is no instance where a tribe has passed from hunting and savagery to quiet agriculture. We have succeeded most imperfectly in attempting this with Indians, in territories whose grazing lands are to those of early Massachusetts as a sloop's main sail is to a pocket handkerchief. When the conflict was gathering, Philip plotted, dissembled, gained time, lied even worse than the Hartford Commissioners did in 1643. How, otherwise, could a good savage have conducted the war? Ulysses would have blamed him, if he had gone into Plymouth and told Winslow that he should attack him on a certain day. Because Philip was dirty, the Massachusetts historian dislikes him. Probably some of the dirt reported clinging to Philip was metaphorical: in any event it did not neutralize his rights as a man. Whether the Creator of men made them all free and equal or no, it is certain that he did not create them clean. Cleanliness is a thing of slow growth and painful administration. Let us treat the savage according to his own ideal, and not constrain him to some impossible standard, derived from weak parts of all the races who have dealt with him.

[1] R. W., Key, p. 64, R. I. H. C.

on each individual native as a solemn duty. We forget that bloody crimes caused by these hereditary and structural differences of government, could not be atoned for by any process satisfactory to both parties. Negotiations, alliances, treaties, so called, were only paltry expedients to bridge over a constantly widening gap between the two systems.[1] If the barbarian could have ignored the vices of his Puritan neighbor, and could have adopted his virtues only, all might have gone well, and the blood of the American might have commingled with the Aryan stream. But generally the worst Indians and the worst colonists dwelt together, then fought themselves apart, and the power of each community was gradually enlisted, until the weaker was exterminated. When the narrowing land contracted so much that the rude hoe could not keep pace with the incoming plow of the agriculturist, the end came.

There was an absolute and actual conflict, not of good and bad men, not of will and the conduct of government, but of race, social structure, and of hereditary civilization. And I use civilization in a large sense including the system developed among the natives of New England; the native Narragansett way of living was as far above that of the dirt-eating Indians, as the Homeric Greeks excelled the Thracians. The stately historian of New England[2] is right, beyond a doubt, when he says that no sentimental admiration of Philip or the splendid Canonchet, should warp our judgment of the mighty issues of this time. Then, as always, the grand features of the contest were not in the heroes, not in the exponents like Sachem Philip, or Church, or Winslow. The essential con-

---

[1] In July, 1673, the court ordered that the Indians, especially young men, running in debt to the English for necessary articles, should be compelled to work it out at reasonable rates (12d. per day), "if they have not else to discharge their just debts." Baylies' Plym., II., 106.

[2] His picture of the infant community in its "general appearance of security, prosperity, sobriety, good order, and content," (III., 137) is true historically, as it is complete rhetorically.

stituents, the permanent symbols of history, were in the social system of Winthrop and Bradford contending with the inferior system of Lenape and Mohawk. The Puritans were uncertain in interpreting the weird light of their exclusive providence. Its flashes lighted them darkly. They groped mainly in painful darkness, as we stumble through the shining circles of the electric lamp into darkness made deeper by its glow. But be assured they made no mistake in their main course and direction. The issue was civil government or savagery, and the Puritans won it. Roger Williams and the Quaker Coddington created a wonderful outgrowth in Rhode Island. This "lively experiment" had results reaching beyond the wildest dreams of its founders. But New England could not have been constructed entirely by Williamses and Quakers. There was a great force existing here, in the might of the native races; it must be met by the counter-force of law and organic government. The gentle-natured Williams—lovely man but pugnacious citizen—and the Quakers, with their vine-like love, clung to the strong natives, when thrust out from Massachusetts by the fierce administration of the Bay, just as the ivy clings to the oak. We shall believe that this love can overcome the tomahawk and firelock, when we see the lamb prevail over the lion. And yet God made them both.

Modern writers either censure our forefathers severely, or say vaguely that there were two sides to the question. True, but unfortunately the Indian's was the losing side always. The more solid justice he carried into a quarrel, the more powder and shot, organized military and accumulated social force, was poured into the scale to overcome him. Justice, there was none. The red and white man differed so essentially that one must kick the beam. There was no standard of balance between the two races. The sentiment of Christianity has never solved this terrible problem of race when government and public interest have been involved. When alien races meet, there must be either the serene justice of superiors, like the Romans blind alike to love and to revenge, or the mild, endogenous love of the Quakers, yielding, but supported by another's strength. There is no middle ground of mixed native and cultivated forces in the history of civilization. We could not reach .the results of this economical discussion without touching upon the greater issues which underlay the mere trade and intercourse of the time. The passions which inspire trade are not the largest, but they are the most certain and continuous in human history.

INDIAN LAND SALES.

Nothing, perhaps, has befogged American moralists more than Indian land sales. Land is worth so much in all solid social systems that every age overrates the value of barbaric uncultivated territory. We forget that the value of every soil is in the atmosphere of intelligence, industry, and virtue diffused over it, by resolute and patient citizens. We fight for land, then give it away to settlers, railways, manufacturers, anyone, who can and will bring in civilization. Were the lands of the Narragansetts and of the Iroquois worth more than those controlled by the imperial governments of England, the United States and France to-day? Yet these powers freely part with land for a slight consideration, and the first colonists almost always lose their ready capital. Those who criticize the colonists for their land transactions with the Indians, in that they purchased it for beads and other articles of trifling value in the eyes of critics, hardly comprehend the time we are studying. Moreover, they have slight knowledge of the power of a currency at any time, or of that force, inherent in the market which compels the movement of property, beyond the control of legislation or treaties. Land was abundant[1] and beads were scarce; coats and gun-

---

[1] "He generally retained his rights of hunting and fishing, and in these consisted the whole value which most of his land had to him before he received pay for it." Palfrey, III., 138.

powder were scarcer yet. To apply the ethics of other systems of living to these transactions is even more silly than the foolishness of the Indians themselves. The man who paid ten shillings for a beaver cap in London was foolish in the eyes of him who wore a knit cap worth one shilling. The furs became more abundant and he got his cap for five shillings. All the colonial trade changes its character in consequence of this fall in the value of beaver. We might say, with as much truth, that the London citizen whenever he bought a cap, cheated a poor Indian out of half its value.

Land titles vary with the social power which occasions them. Boston peninsula was worth so little to the settlers, that they never troubled Chickataubut,[1] the native suzerain to make a deed of it, though he never objected to the occupation. Half a century later in 1685, when Dudley and Audros were shaking the political foundations of the colony, then the citizens thought of the original owners of the soil. They resorted to the living representative of Chickataubut, his grandson Charles Josias, obtaining a deed, which they recorded gravely in 1708, that it might become a corner stone of Suffolk County. This historic evolution is an epitome of the changing process through which Indian lands passed. It was not the soil, it was the things on the soil, which transmuted shell beads into gold.

Purchase of Newport and Rhode Island.

Aquidneck, now lighted by the brilliant villas of Newport, was conveyed in more legitimate and continuous fashion. The "liberty of conscience" men outlawed from Massachusetts, were forced to plant their homes on the most stable political foundation attainable. They extinguished the native titles to the land formally, and it was a curious process revealing the shading and intersecting lines of Indian owner-

---

[1] Mem. His. Bos. (Ellis) I., 249.

ship. Coddington testified in 1677,[1] that in 1636/7 he went to the local Sachem, Wonnumetonomey, to buy the island. "His answer was that Canonicus and Miantonomy were the Chief sachems, and he could not sell the lands; whereupon this deponent with some others went from Aquidneck Island into the Narragansett, and bought the Island of them." Canonicus[2] with a bow and arrow, Miantonomo with an arrow signed the deed, March 24, 1636/7, Roger Williams, Randall Holden, *Mishammoh*, son of Canonicus, witnessing by marks. The consideration was forty fathoms of white beads to be equally divided between Canonicus and Miantonomo. And a further item "that by giveinge by Miantunomus' (hand) ten coates and twenty howes to the present inhabitants, they shall remove themselves off the Island before next winter." In 1638,[3] Wanamataunewit witnesseth that he has "received five fathom of wampum and doe consent to the contents." 6th fifth month, 1638, Ousamequin[4] or Massasoit, the Wampanoag or Pokanoket Sachem of Mount Hope, freely consents that "Coddington and his friends united shall make use of any grasse or trees on yee Maine land on Powakasick side, and doe promise loveinge and just carriage of myselfe and all my men to the said Mr. Coddington and English his friends united to him, havinge received five fathom of wampum as gratuity." All this was by the advice of Williams, who directed them to propitiate all the Indians by every means. We remark that the native prince sells loving carriage and justice for five fathom of beads. May 11, 1639, Miantunnomu[5] receipts for "tenn fathom of wampum peage and one broad cloth coate (as a gratuity) for my paines and travell in removeing of the

---

[1] R. I. Col. R., I., 51.
[2] R. I. Col. Rec., I., 46.
[3] Ibid., p. 47.
[4] R. I. Col. Rec., I., 46.
[5] R. I. Col. Rec., I., p. 48.

natives off the Island of Aquednecke." Three days later Weshaganesett receives five fathom and a coate "in full satisfaction for ground broken up or any other title or claime." Wanimenatoni with the symbol of a snake, inasmuch as he had received previous payments, releases the same claims for five fathoms without any coat. Then it seems that the princely word of Canonicus and of Miantonomo, to free the land of the actual inhabitants for 10 coats and 20 hoes did not hold out. For although Miantonomo had received in May an additional ten fathoms and a fine coat for his paines, he acknowledges, May 22, 1639, the receipt of 23 coats instead of the 10 contracted for, 13 hoes instead of the original 20 to distribute. These transactions complete the transfer of the fair island of Rhode Island. Theorists like Henry George, complaining of modern capitalists and landlords, of the much to a few and the little to the many in these later times, sighing for a return to primitive nature, may take heart. These princely native landowners seem to have given little to actual cultivators and occupants, and to have grasped seigniorage and brokerage with equal greed. Times are changed, and the white broker has somewhat improved upon his red prototype, for he makes but one contract, and generally sticks to it faithfully, if the principal survives to receive his share.

INDIAN POLITY.

This land, this districted portion of the earth's surface was the foundation of a rude polity, which was breaking down and yielding gradually under the pressure of New England society. Much sympathy has been expended upon the native inhabitant; not so much intelligence has been applied to investigate fairly his system of living. We have looked backward, from our system to his, while we should have divested ourselves of prejudices inbred with civilization. We should try to view the barbaric social system, as it looked before the more complex societies, which we call civilized, existed. We are beginning to look into institutions from this point of view, to trace the wonderful development of custom into law, to respect that slow growth of usage, which forms social organisms. How could the Puritan conceive of this intellectual largeness of the social eye, nay, how could he act on a large charity begotten of its discoveries? He regarded each concrete act of importance, as directly inspired by God or the Devil.

The Indian's system was so deficient in the large organs and functions, which we now think essential in a state that the wonder is, it accomplished so much.[1] The French observers, not likely to over-rate any system not their own, compared that of the Iroquois to the organism of a watch, in the nice adjustments of its parts to the ordered movement of the whole.[2] While they condemned justly the barbaric system of punishing crime through one's relatives and friends, instead of through the guilty criminal, yet they admitted that bad crimes were not so common as they were under the splendid imperialism of France.

Wampum marks the passage of ideas into symbols. The belt is arrested literature, a crude germ of that ultimate statement of ideas and abstractions, which evolve in the matured imagination and instructed intelligence of civilized man. The regulated custom of a tribe is the foreshadowing of future law and formulated justice. But the illuminated wampum stops far short of the abstractions conveyed in letters, written words, logical thoughts. So the organism of tribal law and justice stops before it achieves a thoroughly social abstraction, before it subjects the individual to the whole of society. Persons stand for formulated ideas of social justice; personal vengeance must atone for personal wrong. Revenge,[3] the claim-

---

[1] Parkman, Jesuits in North America, p. lxviii.

[2] Parkman, Jesuits in North America, p. lx.

[3] "Among the Iroquis and other Indian tribes generally, the obligation to avenge the murder of a kinsman was universally recognized." Morgan Anc. Society, p. 77.

ing back something for wrongs suffered, underlies the barbaric idea of justice. A child learns directly or by heredity the motive, "I give you this for love." The savage child says, "I give this fruit for that sugar, this blow for that taunt." This direct responsibility, instant revenge for immediate wrong, liability of person to person was the main forming principle of savage communities. There were rude, political, religious, and social obligations, consolidated into tribal government, but underlying these was this earlier and more imperative scheme of accountability. It worked itself out in a clan organization within the tribes.

THE TOTEM SYSTEM.

The Iroquois confederacy[1] was originally in five tribes: Mohawks, Onondagas, etc., and in eight clans, Wolf, Tortoise, etc. A Mohawk Wolf might marry an Oneida Tortoise, or a Mohawk Tortoise, but he could not marry one of his own clan. These clans were not equal; three excelled in rank so much that the traces of the lower ones are almost lost. Each was known by its *totem* mark, tortoise, etc., often tatooed on the skin. The members[2] could elect or depose a sachem or chief; could not marry within their own *totem*; could inherit property mutually; must help and defend each other, redress and avenge wrong; could give names[3] to members; could adopt strangers; and had other privileges and duties. This *totem* system was one of the very oldest human institutions,

---

[1] Parkman, Jesuits in North America, p. IV.
[2] Morgan, Anc. Society, p. 71.
[3] This conferring of names had much significance in savagery, where a man carried his record with him. The personal name of John, borne by a Smith or Brown, indicates no connection with other Smiths. Indian personal names frequently indicated the clan or *totem* of the individual, *i. e.*, some boy-names of the Omaha *totem* "Pigeon Hawk" were "Long Wing," "Hawk balancing itself in the air," "White Eyed Bird." See Morgan, Anc. Society, p. 78.

historic or prehistoric. It[1] has been found in all parts of the world, marking the passage of the lowest tribes into a higher barbaric state. It differed from all other kinds of organization, and it was a grouping force of tremendous power. It was founded in kinship, but it adopted and, as it never intermarried, it gave the extension of adoption to the force of blood and kin. It built up and consolidated barbaric society;[2] it was fitted to rend and destroy the better parts of civilized communities. The New England tribes[3] were not as highly developed as those master barbarians the Iroquois, but they had the same kind of totemic system.[4]

---

[1] "Their most distinct characteristics are, that they mark their bodies with some common mark or *totem*, and that the members of the same group never intermarry; and thus they resembled a Sex rather than any other combination of human beings now familiar to us." Maine, Early Laws and Customs, p. 286.

[2] "Besides their generall subjection to the highest Sachems, to whom they carry presents. They have also particular Protectors under Sachems, to whom they also carry presents, and upon any injury received, and complaint made, these Protectors will revenge it." R. Wms., Key, p. 121, ed. 1827.

[3] Morgan, Anc. Society, p. 173. "Since the Mohegans are organized into gentes (clans), there is a presumption that the Pequots, Narragansetts, and other minor tribes were not only similarly organized, but had the same gentes. The Mohegans have the same three with the Delawares, the Wolf (totem), the Turtle, and the Turkey, each of which is composed of a number of gentes. Descent is in the female line, intermarriage in the gens is forbidden, and the office of sachem is hereditary in the gens, the office passing either from brother to brother, or from uncle to nephew. Among the Pequots and Narragansetts, descent was in the female line." Schoolcraft terms Morgan's *gens* a "totemic system."

[4] The self-ruling qualities in Indian Society have impressed all observers. "An Indian tribe is a singular homogeneous body—socially not politically—and if not disturbed by the intrusion of alien and discordant elements, is susceptible of being governed and controlled with the greatest ease and effect. The public sentiment of an Indian community is absolutely conclusive upon all the members of it." F. A. Walker, then Indian Com., N. A. Rev., CXVI., 365.

THE PURITAN SYSTEM AND THE CONFLICT.

The Puritans, if we consider their ecclesiastical system to be a part of their civil code, which it was in practice, had the most elaborate civic society then prevailing. It was the resultant of Teutonic representation, Judaism, Feudalism and Roman law, all combined. This complex octopus spread its arms about the *totem* of the poor native, tortured him for half a century, and finally crushed him. Mark that many of the acts and customs we ascribe to Indian treachery, or to their tribal and rude national politics, grew out of this peculiar social organism. The object of civil law is to make me testify against my own brother, in behalf of the state; the object of protection under a barbaric *totem*, is to prevent the state or any other power from injuring one of *us*. The intercourse of the two races began with the best traits, the most charitable virtues of either. No community has enough of these for every day life; the supply fails and law reinforces love. This intercourse ended in the vices and worst passions of both Indian and European. It could not have been otherwise, but it is instructive to study the process by which the two races tried to abide together.

The New England savage was a man of the woods, the Puritans would have made him into a peasant, a man of the fields; they did not contemplate in him a citizen, a representative man of the state. This possibility was beyond their ken; this common privilege of citizenship, the slow development of later time, was even beyond the reach of the lower members of their own race. At best, the contact of the two races was a vexed and vexatious question. We must consider the efforts of the New England men, toward a solution, in the light of their own century, and give them credit for an honest effort to make a better man out of the Indian. This effort was made within the narrow limits of their own consciousness, under inevitable conditions, which this century recognizes as the conditions of opposing social systems. The savages were indeed children of a larger growth. Their remarkable patience, stolid endurance under torture, was a factitious virtue, bred out of manners, not out of morals. They had little of what we call moral restraint.[1] Their wills moved within certain inflexible limits of custom, but it was will nevertheless. Passionate in affection, their own children ruled them. Williams asks for a drink of water,[2] his host directs his son eight years old to bring it. The boy refuses, and Williams delivers a moral lecture on the duties of parents and children; the Indian takes a stick to flog the boy into obedience, the boy another to fight it out. The father suffers more than the child in this effort to bring manners to a foreign standard of morals. With this defective moral culture, the Indians were thrown into a complex legal system devised to keep a few rascals from hindering the easy practice of virtue among the better people, the great majority of the colonial community. The whole legal procedure was a dreaded constraint. The patriarchal judgment of Miantonomo,[3] sitting at the gate metaphorically, was better in native eyes than the best rendering of statute[4] and precedent by Winthrop and Bradford. The Indians were tempted in every way; the virtue of the Europeans was not their virtue, the white rascals were preying on them always, while red men were punished for crimes which hardly differed in their eyes from the petty virtues of the whites. Then there was the overwhelming tendency toward injustice to the Indian I have indicated already. For example, Plymouth[5] fines 40s. and condemns to the stocks a cunning citizen of Rehoboth "for goeing into an Indian house, and taking away an Indian child and som goods, in luc of a debt." There is a muddle

---

[1] Parkman, Jesuits in North America, p. lxxviii.
[2] R. Wms., Key, p. 45.
[3] R. I. C. R., I., 107. R. I. tried to meet this, by giving Miantonomo power to "see the Tryal" in matters involving over ten fathoms.
[4] See R. I. C. R., II., 362, in 1670.
[5] Col. Rec., III., 74.

of barbarism and the forms of civilization; debt lawfully incurred, says Pecksniff; child-ravishing and plunder, says every man in any age. How many such wrongs went unpunished; how many similar, but not indictable offences rankled in the Wampanoag and Narragansett bosom, when they stood at bay in the Swamp fight? Wherever there was a difference between man and man, it was against the native. Rhode Island enacted in 1666,[1] that no Indian should keep a hog with cut marks in his ears; nor could any one sell a sheep, swine or other skin, without the ears, under severe penalties. The inference was plain that Indians would steal pigs, if they could, and the colonists thus prevented their availing of the opportunity. But what a condition for the race, once haughty and proprietary, now dropping into subjection after 30 years of joint occupancy. The pressure of the superior race was constant and cumulating. In 1664 Plymouth fines five Indians 20s. each for misdemeanors; in 1665 five Indians owe £5; in 1668 £25 is brought forward as "remaines of the forty pound from the Indians."[2] They were condemned by the General Court to work out debts at 12d. per day. Statistics prove nothing directly, but they indicate the facts which go to the proof. In seven years from 1661–68, at Plymouth there are fifteen prosecutions against Indians for trespass and stealing, while there were only three prosecutions against whites for trespass on the Indians. These dates are all in the crucial time, when the aboriginal mind was seething and inflaming itself for the final revolt. Nevertheless the colonists tried with all their might to work out the problem according to their own ideas of justice and fairness.[3]

---

[1] R. I. C. R., II., 172.
[2] Plymouth Col. Rec., VIII., 111, 113, 124.
[3] Rhode Island voted in 1673 to try an Indian for murder, by a jury of six Englishmen and six Indians, and that Indian testimony should be received. I do not find that the experiment was repeated. R. I. C. R., II., 509.

Behind all these civil processes, a dark institution older by centuries, loomed up and perplexed the councils of the jurists. The blood feud and vendetta meant treachery and vengeance to the ecclesiastical lawyer of Massachusetts, but to an outraged Indian it meant swift and certain justice. Citations from Samuel and all the Jewish law-givers would not convince a burly brave that he should not avenge his wounded honor, whenever he could, upon any individual of these powerful interlopers. A man bearing a hatchet in his head[1] and sorrow in his heart would not reason long in texts from the word of the Lord, when he met an enemy in the dark, or surprised him asleep in a lonely homestead. The colonists tried to soothe the pride of the natives by carrying the principle of the honor-price into their statutes.[2] Torts[3] went back to their original source to satisfy the crude justice of the aboriginal mind.

THE RELIGIOUS CONFLICT.

We have sketched the economic and civil phases of aboriginal-colonial life, and it is not too satisfactory, either to

---

[1] O'Callaghan, Doc'y. Col. N. Y., VII., 44.

[2] As early as 1645, certain persons are fined by the men of Plymouth one-half bushel of corn "for affray with Vssamaquine and men." Plym. Col. Rec., II., 89. "1664. It appearing that Nathaniel York did strike Obediah, the Indian, several stripes, he is satisfied from him by *half a bushel of corn*, and his fine is left to the town's determination." Thompson, Long Island, I., 314. And in Plym. Col. Rec., V., p. 31. 1669, one Mathews is "fined for beating Indian Ned, the King's peace 3s. 4d. for abuse said Indian, and his charges Mathews ordered to pay him 14s." Mark the difference in the nature of the two fines, one is to vindicate the State in an ordinary civil offence, the other is strictly an honor-price awarded to the Indian to recompense him for his personal injury.

[3] "If therefore the criterion of a *delict*, wrong, or *tort*, be that the person who suffers it, and not the State, is conceived to be wronged, it may be asserted that in the infancy of jurisprudence the citizen depends for protection against violence or fraud not on the Law of Crime, but on the Law of Tort." Maine, Ancient Law, p. 359.

the seventeenth century or to the nineteenth. The religious phase of this life was worse. Perhaps no change in the mental atmosphere of the two centuries is relatively so great as the alteration in our purely religious consciousness. Philosophers and theologians then regarded a barbaric religion as a mummery or an abomination. Few intelligent persons now would look upon the rudest man in any sincere act of worship, without a feeling of awe and respect. In 1646,[1] the Massachusetts by a positive act, forbid the natives to worship their false gods, *i. e.*, the Puritan Devil. They laid severe penalties against blasphemy, defining it to be the denial of their god, Jehovah. It is true while wampum was current and land abundant that the practically minded sachems would not regard these restrictions as vital. All people have a way of keeping their religions in abeyance, while pushing for the main chance; but none the less the inbred beliefs of centuries abide, and do their work in the fulness of time. Human desires represented in trade are common, prevalent like shoal water; the desires of the soul are deep and living springs, revealing themselves when the surface ponds are dry. When proprietary possession waned, when barbaric commodities were superseded by civilized thrift, when sons and cousins toiled in enforced servitude, when, in 1660 to 1670, the ancestral money ceased to command the market, then the Indian must have brooded over the wrongs done to his outraged faith. He had found that the garments[2] of civilization did not always cover an honest heart; was the Jehovah of the

---

[1] "No Indian shall at any time paw waw, or pforme outward worship to their false gods, or yᵉ devill." This was after minute provisions against blasphemy, defined as "obstinate deniing yᵉ true God, or his creation or government of yᵉ world." Col. Rec. Mass., II., 177.

[2] Ganett, alias Wequascooke, complains to the Court of Connecticut, of "such men that weare hats and cloaths like Englishmen, but have dealt with us like wolves and bears." Col. Rec. Conn., 1667, p. 529. Coat-men was a common designation of the English among the Indians.

powder-horn surely a better god than the Great Spirit or Spirits[1] of the clouds?

The effort of John Eliot[2] is one of the noblest monuments of Christian faith and devotion in all history. Whatever came of it, however meagre the result, however poor a creature was made in the praying Indian, the devotion and Christ-like trust of Eliot and his missionaries, was a mighty thing. The more sagacious colonists doubted the whole movement, but Eliot worked on and prayed. Whatever became of the poor native converts, he made New England better for all time. Eliot preached in the Indian tongue, but made his first prayer in English, not being familiar enough with the strange dialect to trust his emotions to it. A puzzled native who asked the apostle whether God would understand a prayer in the Indian dialect, penetrated deeper into the essence of things than he knew. The lips pray, but

---

[1] History varies, as observers vary. Mr. Parkman, certainly the best individual authority says, (Jesuits in North America, lxxvii), "The Indian belief, if developed, would have developed into a system of polytheism." A late writer, Mr. Doyle (Eng. Col's in Amer., p. 14), says, "The belief in one overruling spirit, and also in the personal existence of the various powers of nature, is established by a wide consensus of opinion."

[2] After about thirty years trial of Eliot's experiment, Philip's war broke out. Then there were seven tolerably well-established, tolerably christianized villages of praying Indians. Seven others were in a crude way working toward this standard. Some left the villages and took part with Philip. This occasioned a panic among the colonists and a wild prejudice against them all. After the war, the stated places for Indian Church settlements were reduced to four; there were other temporary stations. There were ten stations in Plymouth Colony, ten at the Vineyard. five at Nantucket. In 1687, President Mather says there were in New England, six churches of baptized Indians. In 1698 there was reported at Natick a church of seven native men and three women with a native minister ordained by Eliot; in the village were fifty-nine men, fifty-one women and seventy children. Up to 1733, all the town officers were Indians. In 1792, there was only one Indian family. In 1846, the two hundredth anniversary of Eliot's first service, a girl of sixteen was the only known native descendant at Natick, other stations lasted a little longer, with life still more forlorn. Dr. Ellis' account, Mem. Hist. Boston, I., 271-74.

the heart speaketh. The god of the Puritan consciousness sympathized little with the deities controlling Indian life, however earnest souls like Eliot and Williams might labor to negotiate an alliance of the two unseen powers. There is a tract,[1] "Christenings make not Christians," written by Williams, long lost, and lately discovered in the British Museum. Though mainly a polemic against ritualism of all kinds, it is catholic, and throws light on the actual life of that time. It was written in 1645, just as Eliot's work began. It is plain that Williams, knowing more of native life and thought, foresaw more clearly than the Massachusetts men, and especially the English Puritans, could see, the difficulties surrounding Indian regeneration, spiritual or temporal. The change[2] in his eyes must not only convert them in the technical sense, it must remodel the whole structure of the men and their race. It was in the golden days, after the Pequot war, while aboriginal-colonial intercourse was at the flood, while it was mutual and both parties benefitting thereby, that Miantonomo and the Connecticut sachem inclined toward the Christian way. Later on, in 1654, Ninigret and the Narragansett

---

[1] "They (the People of America) are intelligent, many very ingenuous, plain-hearted, inquisitive and prepared with many convictions." Under this caption, a discourse concerning the Indian's conversion, we find, "For it is not a forme, nor the change of one forme into another, a finer and a finer, and yet more fine, that makes a man a convert, I mean such a convert as is acceptable to God in Jesus Christ. . . . "Why, then, if this be *conversion*, and you have such a *key* of *Language*, and such a dore of *opportunity* in the knowledge of the country and the inhabitants, why proceed you not? . . . In matters of Earth, men will helpe to spell out each other, but in matters of Heaven (to which the soule is naturally so averse), how far are the eares of man hedged up from listening to all improper Language?" R. I. Hist. Tracts, No. 14, pp. 10, 13, 18. The whole tract is open minded and far in advance of the prevailing dogmas and prejudices of the time.

[2] "The said Sachem, and the chief of his people, discoursed by themselves of keeping the Englishman's day of worship, which I could easily have brought the country to, but that I was persuaded, and am, that God's way is first to turne a soule from its Idolls both of heart, worship and conversation. . . ." R. Wms., Key, p. 117.

sachems begged Williams to intercede with the king in England, "that they might not be forced from their religion, and for not changing their religion, be invaded by war; for they said they were daily visited with threatenings by Indians that came from about the Massachusetts, that if they would not pray they should be destroyed by war."[1] All successful "conversions" have been hastened by the temporal power. The sword of state was in the hands of men who prayed, traded, and fought—men of many affairs. Land was desirable and the Narragansetts held some of the best in the colonies. The Great Pettiquamscutt Purchase was made by Massachusetts men in 1657, the Atherton purchases in 1659, all in that country. Ninigret feared the approaching Christian who prayed so often and struck so hard in the fight, and whose appetite for land knew no satiety. Probably the praying Indians were not the best native stock. The men who wore the old clothes that Eliot carried to Natick tied to his saddle crupper, were not the men to make a new nation or to save an old one. If we try to think so, certainly Philip and Ninigret thought otherwise. Sausamon, one of the converts, informed the colonists of the rising conspiracy and Philip's men waylaid and killed him. When the revolt broke out, some of the praying Indians took the war-path with their blood relatives; after the war, these poor savages halting between two ways, neither Christian nor barbarian, declined and dwindled into decay. This was the fate of those who adopted a mongrel Christianity. The proud Narragansetts mingled their blood with that of negro slaves, and the result was not better. The great Jesuit Missions in the North West, inspired by a profound spirit of devotion, worked with all the skill of that powerful Order, produced no permanent results. We have treated Narragansetts and Wampanoags mainly, for they were the chief tribes; the principle was the same throughout all New England. The natives ceased to be fierce barbarians to become coarse dependents of an alien civilization.

---

[1] R. W. to Gen. Ct., Mass. R. I. Col. Rec., I., 292.

The little shell bead with which we began is the symbol of the rise and fall of aboriginal-colonial life. Trade means to tread. With the wampum beads, red and white men trod along familiar paths in ways easy to both. Individual man met his neighbor, prompted by a common universal passion. Not for gain merely, do men strive so hard and endure so much in the intercourse of trade. Common desires draw men together in a commerce of love; gold or wampum is a symbol of that love, which if not altogether pure is peaceable, and is on the whole healthful. This kind of intercourse can serve only between man and man. When communities meet, systems clash. Land settlement, the foundation of property; civil law, the instrument of social order; religion, the outward form of the soul's being; all combine to weave the complicated and involved tissues of national or race life. In the fulness of time, this providential product, this evolution of the centuries comes. It meets another and inferior system. The barbarian reels under the shock and his system crumbles into dust, which feeds the growth of a new and stronger race.

PUBLICATIONS OF THE
JOHNS HOPKINS UNIVERSITY
BALTIMORE.

I. **American Journal of Mathematics.**
   J. J. SYLVESTER, Editor. Quarterly. 4to. Volume VII in progress. $5 per volume.

II. **American Chemical Journal.**
   I. REMSEN, Editor. Bi-monthly. 8vo. Volume VI in progress. $3 per volume.

III. **American Journal of Philology.**
   B. L. GILDERSLEEVE, Editor. Quarterly. 8vo. Volume V in progress. $3 per volume.

IV. **Studies from the Biological Laboratory.**
   Including the Chesapeake Zoölogical Laboratory. H. N. MARTIN, Editor, and W. K. BROOKS, Associate Editor. 8vo. Volume III in progress. $5 per volume.

V. **Studies in Historical and Political Science.**
   H. B. ADAMS, Editor. Monthly. 8vo. Volume II in progress. $3 per volume.

VI. **Contributions to Logic.**
   C. S. PEIRCE, Editor. Little, Brown & Co., Boston, Publishers.

VII. **Johns Hopkins University Circulars.**
   Containing reports of scientific and literary work in progress in Baltimore. 4to. Vol. I, $5; Vol. II, $3; Vol. III in progress. $1 per year.

VIII. **Annual Report.**
   Presented by the President to the Board of Trustees, reviewing the operations of the University during the past academic year.

IX. **Annual Register.**
   Giving the list of officers and students, and stating the regulations, etc., of the University. *Published at the close of the academic year.*

The *University Circulars, Annual Report,* and *Annual Register* will be sent by mail for one dollar per annum.

Communications in respect to exchanges and remittances may be sent to the Johns Hopkins University (Publication Agency), Baltimore, **Maryland.**

LAW BOOKS
PUBLISHED BY
CUSHINGS & BAILEY,
BALTIMORE, MD.

ALEXANDER'S BRITISH STATUTES IN FORCE IN MARYLAND. 1 vol. 8vo	$10 00
BARROLL'S MARYLAND CHANCERY PRACTICE. 1 vol. 8vo.	3 00
BLAND'S " " REPORTS. 3 vols. 8vo.	15 00
BUMP'S FEDERAL PROCEDURE. 1 vol. 8vo	6 50
" FRAUDULENT CONVEYANCES. Third Edition. 1 vol. 8vo	6 50
EVANS' MARYLAND COMMON LAW PRACTICE. 1 vol. 8vo.	4 00
HINKLEY & MAYER ON LAW OF ATTACHMENT IN MARYLAND. 1 vol. 8vo	3 00
MARYLAND DIGEST, by NORRIS, BROWN & BRUNE. Comprising Harris & McHenry, 4 vols. Harris & Johnson, 7 vols. Harris & Gill, 2 vols. Gill & Johnson, 12 vols. Bland's Chancery, 3 vols	10 00
" DIGEST, by STOCKETT, MERRICK & MILLER. Comprising Gill, 9 vols. Maryland, 1—8 inc. Johnson's Chancery, 4 vols	10 00
" DIGEST, by COHEN & LEE. Comprising 9—20 inc. Maryland	10 00
" DIGEST, by BURGWYN. Comprising 21 to 45 inc. Maryland	10 00
POE'S PLEADINGS AND PRACTICE. 2 vols. Vol. 1, Pleading. Second edition in press. " 2, Practice	7 00
GROUND RENTS IN MARYLAND. By LEWIS MAYER, ESQ., of the Baltimore Bar. 1 vol	1 50
MARYLAND REPORTS. 60 Vols. 1851 to 1883. Per vol	4 00

A few *complete* sets of Maryland Reports on hand at present, comprising:

    Harris & McHenry's Reports, 4 vols.;—Harris & Johnson's Reports, 7 vols.;—Harris & Gill's Reports, 2 vols.;—Gill & Johnson's Reports, 12 vols.;—Gill's Reports, 9 vols.;—Maryland Reports, 60 vols.;—Bland's Chancery Reports, 3 vols.;—Johnson's Chancery Reports, 4 vols.;—101 vols. For sale cheap.

They also keep a large and complete stock of Law, Classical, Medical and Miscellaneous Publications, which they offer for sale at low prices.

    Agents for Sale of the Publications of the Johns Hopkins University.

JUST PUBLISHED.

THE LAW OF HEREDITY,

By W. K. BROOKS,

Associate in Biology, Johns Hopkins University.

1 Volume, 12mo. Cloth, $2.00.

WHAT THE PRESS SAYS OF IT.

Asa Gray in the Andover Review.

An Essay which aims to succeed where Darwin failed, to correct some of his judgments, to explain away difficulties in the theory of natural selection which he confessed his inability to meet, and especially which is to account for variation, which, if we remember rightly, Darwin thought unaccountable, is certainly a very ambitious undertaking. But the attempt is made with a full knowledge of the actual condition of the questions involved, and the case is argued with real ability by a naturalist who has already made a mark in investigation and shown aptitude in speculation. One sees the handiwork of a trained and accomplished zoölogist, not of an amateur, who usually shows his want of mastery of the subject alike when he hits and when he misses the mark.

Amer. Jour. of Science.

Darwin himself would have have hailed Mr. Brooks's version as an improvement.

New York Times.

It is extremely probable that Mr. W. K. Brooks has discovered a highly important factor overlooked by Darwin. It is quite certain to make a stir, and stamps Mr. W. K. Brooks as a biologist of very extraordinary promise. His treatise is cause for pride to the United States.

Medical Tribune.

A careful perusal of this work will give the reader a clear idea of the true meaning of Heredity. We believe the time is not far distant when all scientific men will admit that too little attention has been paid to the conditions by which the human race might be improved physically, morally, and mentally. This is the best work on this that has yet been published and we cannot too strongly urge its careful study upon our readers.

The Science Record.

We would cordially commend this work to all who are interested in the philosophy of biology, whether as special students or in a more general manner, for it is one of the most suggestive works which have appeared since the first publication of Darwin's Origin of Species.

Popular Science Monthly.

This work combines in a very unusual degree the two traits that are so rarely found to coexist in scientific books: it is both original and independent in its views, and is at the same time a most lucid and popular presentation of its subject. . . . There is more than plausibility, more even than probability, in this idea, and those who look critically into the evidence adduced by the author can hardly fail to recognize that he has seized upon an important principle in this field of investigation.

☞ *By mail prepaid to any address on receipt of price.*

JOHN MURPHY & CO., Publishers,

182 BALTIMORE STREET, BALTIMORE.

11 MURRAY STREET, NEW YORK.

www.ingramcontent.com/pod-product-compliance
Lightning Source LLC
Chambersburg PA
CBHW031551110426
42739CB00039B/1110